ALSO BY DON DELILLO

NOVELS

Americana

End Zone

Great Jones Street

Ratner's Star

Players

Running Dog

The Names

White Noise

Libra

Mao II

Underworld

The Body Artist

Cosmopolis

PLAYS

The Day Room

Valparaiso

DON DeLILLO

LOVE-LIES-BLEEDING

A PLAY

PICADOR

First published 2005 by Scribner, NY, USA

First published in Great Britain in paperback 2006 by Picador
an imprint of Pan Macmillan Ltd
Pan Macmillan, 20 New Wharf Road, London N1 9RR
Basingstoke and Oxford
Associated companies throughout the world
www.panmacmillan.com

ISBN-13: 978-0-330-43955-8
ISBN-10: 0-330-43955-3

1 3 5 7 9 8 6 4 2

A CIP catalogue record for this book is available from
the British Library.

Printed and bound in Great Britain by
Mackays of Chatham plc, Chatham, Kent

All Pan Macmillan titles are available from
www.panmacmillan.com
or from Bookpost by telephoning +44 (0)1624 677237

To Nan Graham

LOVE-LIES-BLEEDING

ALEX	a man, seventy
TOINETTE	a woman, late fifties
SEAN	a man, thirty-five
LIA	a woman, early thirties

Two actors appear as Alex. One plays the character in three episodes that precede the main action. The other plays Alex *in extremis*, a helpless figure attached to a feeding tube.

A spacious room in an old house, remotely located. The set is spare and semi-abstract, with subdued lighting and a few pieces of well-worn furniture, including a sofa. There is also a metal stand equipped with an intravenous feeding setup.

In several scenes a limited sector of the stage functions as playing area.

ACT ONE

Scene 1

Alex and Lia, one year before the main action of the play.

He is haggard, after a stroke, seated in a wheelchair, stage right, isolated from the room set, which is in near darkness. His speech is labored. Lia sits in close proximity, a food bowl within reach.

Across the stage, in scant light, barely visible, there is the sitting figure of a man.

ALEX

I saw a dead man on the subway once. I was ten or eleven, riding with my father. The man was in a corner seat, across the aisle. Only a few people in the car. A dead man sits there. This is the subway. You don't know about this. Nobody looks at anybody else. He sits there, and I'm the only one that sees him. I see him so clearly now I could almost tell you things about his life. My father was reading the newspaper. He liked to follow the horses. He analyzed the charts. He studied the race results. There weren't too many things he followed, my father. Horse races and prizefights. There was a column he always read. If I thought about it long enough, I could tell you the columnist's name.

LIA

And the man. Across the aisle.

ALEX

Nobody paid him the slightest mind. Another sleeping rider, by their dim lights. I watched him steadily. I examined him. I was fixated. When the train rocked. *(Pause.)* I'm thinking how he sat. He sat against the bulkhead, partly, at the end of the car. When the train rocked, he got bounced around a little and I thought he might topple to the floor. His mouth was open. His face, I swear, it was gray. There wasn't any question in my mind. Dead. All life drained out of him. But in a way I can't explain, it didn't seem strange or forbidding. It seemed forbidding but not in a way that threatened me personally. I accepted what I saw. A rider on the train, going breakneck through the tunnel. It scared me to think he might topple to the floor. That was forbidding. He could have been riding all day. Gray like an animal. He belonged to a different order of nature. The first dead man I'd ever seen and there's never been anyone since who has looked more finally and absolutely dead.

LIA

And your father. What did he do? Did he alert someone when the train reached the next station?

ALEX

I don't know. I don't know if I told him. The memory ends here. I draw a total blank. This is the subway. He's reading the sports pages. The column he's reading is part boldface, part regular type, and I can see the face of the columnist in the little photo set into the type. He has a slick mustache. A racetrack mustache.

LIA

Can you tell me his name?

ALEX

His name will come to me in a minute.

Scene 2

Present time. Lights up on the sitting figure. This is Alex, after a massive second stroke. The rest of the room remains dark.

Alex is motionless in a straight-backed chair with arms. It is now possible to see that he is attached to hydration and feeding tubes that extend from a metal stand next to the chair. His eyes are open, mouth open slightly. His hair is cropped. He is clean shaven and neatly dressed—casual pants and shirt, new pair of running shoes.

Lights up on entire room. Toinette and Sean are situated some distance from the sitting figure.

TOINETTE
I don't like sharing a toilet.

SEAN
Maybe I can use the shed.

TOINETTE
Nothing personal.

SEAN
Or dig a hole somewhere.

TOINETTE
What will she say?

9

SEAN
You know what she'll say.

TOINETTE
I don't know her. I know her for half a day.

SEAN
I don't know her much longer.

TOINETTE
You've been here before.

SEAN
Once. After the first stroke. He was home from the hospital.
She was looking after him, very capably, without help. That's
what she wanted then and that's what she wants now.

TOINETTE
Do you think she has any idea?

SEAN
Tell her.

TOINETTE
You tell her.

SEAN
You must have shared a toilet with Alex. Somewhere along the
way.

TOINETTE
We shared many things. We exhausted each other. We shared
our exhaustion.

SEAN

She does everything one person can do for another. A male fantasy of the caring woman. But not really. She's not a little house sparrow. She's smart and tough. Stubborn too.

TOINETTE

Finally what we shared was silence. The entire last year. Everything became internal. Shapeless and motionless. Vaguely sinister. Each of us wishing the other dead in a car crash. I'd sit and study that look of his. Angry and dangerous. Always a question in it. He's puzzled by something.

SEAN (IN ALEX'S VOICE)

I'm probing, I'm searching. Trying to figure out exactly what it is that makes me want to tear out your liver and use it in a painting.

TOINETTE

Our car crashes were different. In my mind, Alex was the only victim. Lying there looking okay, actually, sort of presentably dead.

SEAN

The crash in his mind. What?

TOINETTE

Three or four cars. Nine or ten dead. My friends, colleagues, secret lovers. And I'm in the middle of it, smashed and burnt. All right, I wanted him dead at times. But not scattered into smoky little pieces.

SEAN

That's the difference between men and women.

TOINETTE

That look became a fixed look. We'd seen the last of our living, breathing days and nights.

SEAN

But you're here. Because—tell me.

TOINETTE

There were times, I swear, when we were living in the same skin. That's how I remember it and that's what I want to believe. Makes it easier to understand how we could live as enemies, off and on, for as long as we did. I'm here to be with him, that's all. I want to be close—close as we can get, he and I. I've been here before. You know this.

SEAN

No, I don't know this.

TOINETTE

Couple of days. Long before Lia. Maybe it had a mellowing effect.

SEAN

Why don't I know this? I thought we talked, you and I.

TOINETTE

It was six or seven years ago, and many years after he and I had lost contact. The old furies were not so intense. I guess we both felt this, telepathically. He called out of nowhere. This is nowhere, isn't it? Said come visit for a few days.

SEAN

What happened?

TOINETTE

I don't know. What happened?

SEAN

Did you make reparations? Talk in the same old way. Sleep in the same old bed.

TOINETTE

Why so interested?

SEAN

I'm interested in his life.

TOINETTE

Get your own.

SEAN

He's my father.

TOINETTE

Look at him.

Sean does not look.

Scene 3

Toinette, Sean and Lia. The sitting figure, as in previous scene.

LIA

The lightning season here is late July, early August. Storms appear late afternoon. You see them way off in the mountains, one, then another, sort of crawling down the sky, too far off to be audible yet. A storm may fade and die long before it gets here, and another storm approaches, and then another begins to build somewhere else. One day the light changed quickly and there was a charge in the air. I got him into the wheelchair and took him out to the porch and sat him there, and we waited. When the storm hit, I swear he knew it. The lightning was very near, cloud to ground, and I counted the seconds between the lightning and the thunder and calculated distances. The larger streaks carried a glow that lit up the grasses and scrub. His eyes grew wider and he knew it. I counted aloud and when the thunder hit, or before it hit, before it hit, his hands came up off the chair. His head raised up and he was in awe, I know he was—purest living wonder.

TOINETTE

That was a great thing to do. To think of that. To take him outside and let him experience that.

SEAN

It was a tremendous thing to do.

14

LIA

Sometimes it rains all night and in the morning there's so much mud I have to put down boards to get to the car.

SEAN

But what he's showing is pure reflex. The storm is a powerful stimulus. He's showing meaningless body response. There's no awareness, no consciousness. He's not aware of you or me or anything else. He isn't conscious. And he isn't Alex. Eyes open. This means nothing. Eyes blinking. Means nothing. Hands moving. Nothing. He can't think. He doesn't know what you're saying to him. You are not Lia. He is not Alex.

Scene 4

Toinette and Lia. The sitting figure, eyes closed.

TOINETTE
Then the baby came.

LIA
I don't need to hear this.

TOINETTE
We'd just started something, he and I. Then he called me. I was slightly, at the time, delirious. I was deranged in the best sense, living and breathing on one of the moons of Jupiter. Then he called me. The memory is so clear I see myself standing in the room. I lived in one room. Holding the telephone.
     He said, You'll never guess what she did.
     I said, Who?
     He said, My wife.
     I said, What?
     I was twenty-two years old.
     I said, What?

LIA
You knew he had a wife.

TOINETTE
I knew he had a wife. I knew the marriage was lost at sea.
     I said, What?

He said, She just had a baby.
Then he laughed.

LIA

Then you laughed.

TOINETTE

I don't think so.

LIA

Why tell me this?

TOINETTE

That's what we're here for. To tell each other things.

LIA

Why not tell Sean?

TOINETTE

Sean knows.

LIA

Because he was the baby.

TOINETTE

He was the baby. Shouldn't he know? Sean wants to know everything his father said and did. He's a little twisted on the subject. He asked me once about his father's sexual method. His tone and style. What he liked, where he liked.

LIA

And you said.

TOINETTE

Whatever you would have said. That's what I said. But it's not as bad as it sounds. Sean says things because he believes he's expected to say them. He says what a person like him would say. There's something generic about Sean. He's like someone who's like him.

LIA

Let's not analyze. I'm not interested in that. And that's a long time ago, all of it.

TOINETTE

The world was flat, sweet and simpleminded. Suddenly, look, a baby.

Lia takes a soft cloth and moistens the sitting figure's lips.

LIA

I know why you're here. Both of you.

TOINETTE

Of course you do.

Scene 5

Toinette and Sean. The sitting figure, eyes closed, head slumped.

TOINETTE
Look at him. What does he look like?

Sean does not look.

SEAN
She shaves him every day. Cuts his hair every few days whether it's growing or not. I don't know if hair grows in his situation. He looks like that guy who had a kids' show on TV. Mister somebody. Mister Mister Mister.

TOINETTE
Mister Ed.

SEAN
Mister Ed was a horse.

TOINETTE
Mister Ed was a horse. Why does that sound so evocative? Like a line from the *Iliad*.

SEAN
Cuts his fingernails. Then she buffs.

TOINETTE

I'm standing here looking at him and I realize I haven't thought about this nearly as long and deeply as I should have.

SEAN

Speaking only for yourself.

TOINETTE

We're here to do something so far beyond our experience— mine anyway—that I haven't even tried to confront it. Look at the running shoes.

SEAN

I like the running shoes. I try not to read too much into them.

TOINETTE

He looks like an old man in a supermarket somewhere, lost in Frozen Foods.

SEAN

He's asleep in his shopping cart. He climbed in and went to sleep. Said the hell with it. You're the one who has to tell her.

TOINETTE

Nobody has to tell her. She knows.

SEAN

We have to get her explicit consent.

TOINETTE

It won't happen.

SEAN

It has to. She's his wife.

TOINETTE

She's one of his wives. I'm one of his wives. We're just pussy.
You're his blood root. The only son. The only child. His descen-
dant. You come from him.

SEAN

Courts favor the spouse.

TOINETTE

This isn't a public matter. This is small and quiet.

SEAN

We need her involvement. It doesn't have to be active. But she
has to know. She has to give her consent. It works better on
every level. Otherwise.

TOINETTE

We're not going to get her consent.

SEAN

Otherwise.

TOINETTE

We're not going to get her consent.

SEAN

You have to tell her. Tell her. The two of you. The women.
Alone.

Scene 6

Toinette and Lia. The sitting figure, as in previous scene.

LIA

Sometimes I forget. I come back from somewhere and walk into the room. I see him sitting here. I have to pause and gather myself. I think, Who is this man? How did this happen? I don't know how this happened to me. Is this how I want to live, day after day, all day, into the night?

TOINETTE

You marry someone so much older, something like this has to happen. The feeling you have is only natural. And it's only a moment, isn't it, now and then?

LIA

It's only a moment. And it passes. But I want to take hold of my head. I want to crush it.

TOINETTE

How long has he been like this?

LIA

Seven months.

TOINETTE

Immobile. Completely helpless.

LIA

I have some training in this kind of work. I have some abilities. But I don't know if you can imagine what's involved. Just getting him into bed. I want him in his bed at night. But just that one thing. And there are endless things.

TOINETTE

What we do for someone else, someone we love. It's the truest kind of human beauty. *(Pause.)* Only lose those shoes. Find him a pair of sick man's shoes.

LIA

We used to climb into the hills. Climb for hours without a word. We felt such happiness. He had enormous endurance. We'd stop to drink water and he'd take my hand and put it to his heart. His heart beating insanely on the steepest climbs. His heart jumping out of his chest. It scared me. He laughed and poured water on my head.

TOINETTE

What else?

LIA

What else. A single drifting hawk about a million miles away.

TOINETTE

Why are we clustered around him? Not because he's a loving husband and father whose lifelong devotion. Not because he's the patriarch of a teeming family. Look at us. The three survivors. Bare bones in triplicate. Not because we feel indebted in any way—I don't. Or morally, somehow, obligated—I'm not. Or need his final blessing—too late for that. It's much more ele-mental, isn't it? We're here to help him die.

LIA
He's not ready yet. Go home and work on your speech.

Scene 7

Room set is dark. Lights up on lectern, downstage, left. Sean enters and takes up a position behind the lectern.

SEAN

You knew my father better than I did, most of you. Maybe I knew him in a deeper way—deeper and stranger. When I was a kid, I never called him Dad straight-out, face to face. I didn't have a name for him. Think how strange that is. Then, again, I didn't see him much and this made the business of names a little less awkward. He was a large figure, out there somewhere, with hair and teeth. He was a force in people's lives. You know this. And I began to know this, gradually, over time. He drew people in. Friend who picks him up at airport. Friend who lends him money. Friend whose wife whatever. All right, so what? *De mortuis nil nisi bonum.* He was an artist. Look at his work. The work's what matters, isn't it? When he gave up easel painting, finally, to do land art in the West, it seemed he'd found his calling. I'm sure many of you felt that way. A scale to match the man. He carried all the signs and measures—he was the measure of a man who did great and famous work. But he wasn't great and he wasn't famous. And we share, somewhere lurking, some of us, a small, dismal pleasure in this knowledge. Don't we? I think we do. He absorbed certain people, consumed and absorbed them. You know this. Those he didn't consume he left standing in the street somewhere. Say nothing but good of the dead.

Scene 8

Toinette, Sean and Lia. The sitting figure, head up, eyes shut.

LIA
How he dies. This is what we live with forever.

SEAN
True.

TOINETTE
All of us.

LIA
True.

TOINETTE
End his pain.

LIA
What pain?

SEAN
End his pain. We can live with this, can't we? Euthanasia.
Good death.

LIA
His death at your hands. This is what you'll live with. What's
your method? Injection, asphyxiation. You think there's such a

thing as a good death. So do I. It's when the living do not inter-fere according to their needs. Let him die in his time.

TOINETTE
When is his time?

LIA
No one knows.

TOINETTE
All these months. How much longer?

LIA
I prefer not knowing. Did you bring the canister? Do you have the mask, the tubing, the carbon monoxide? Is that what they use? Or something else.

SEAN
His condition has a name for a good reason.

LIA
I don't want to hear that name.

TOINETTE
What name?

SEAN
Persistent vegetative state.

LIA
I don't want to hear that name. It's stupid and cruel.

SEAN
His brain has shrunk. We know this. The CAT scan told us. The situation is hopeless. There is no hope.

TOINETTE
Let him find peace.

LIA
There's no peace when someone dies. There's nothing. Whatever he feels now, this is who he is. This is Alex Macklin. You have no right to take this from him.

TOINETTE
Let him rest. Please.

LIA
Your peace, your rest.

TOINETTE
Think of the long nights. You know that feeling. Maybe you don't.

SEAN
Can't sleep.

TOINETTE
Can't sleep. Can't control the flow of thought. Every thought is troubled. There's a fear you can't dispel.

SEAN
You're in a state of low resistance.

TOINETTE
You're not fully conscious. Not armored. I have these nights. There's a helplessness, a terror. Is it possible this is where he is, if he's anywhere?

SEAN

Only it's all the time. Not an hour or two some random night.

LIA

I don't want to talk about this.

TOINETTE

What else is there?

SEAN

This is all there is.

TOINETTE

We're here.

SEAN

Why are we here?

LIA

He has a life, still.

SEAN

Life is heat, it's motion.

TOINETTE

Can you possibly believe this is what he wanted? This man.

LIA

I have to go inside and change the bedsheets now. This is what I do.

Scene 9

Toinette, Sean and Lia. The sitting figure, as in previous scene.

LIA

The first attack set something loose in him. Once he was able to speak, he talked in a way he'd never done before. I thought, This is his true voice. I thought, Every word he speaks carries a lifetime of feeling.

TOINETTE

Did he know what was coming?

LIA

The second stroke. It came. The massive insult to the brain. But he's not gone. He's there. I can see him in there. And he can hear me when I speak to him, slowly and clearly. Hearing is the last faculty to collapse. At times he moans but not in pain. It isn't pain. I know this.

TOINETTE

I want to believe you.

LIA

Do you understand he is in a place that is blessed by death? He is in last life. This is exalted time. No one has the right to deprive him of this.

SEAN

He moans. But not in pain. You know this.

LIA

Yes.

SEAN

Let me tell you something you don't know. He moans—
because a feeding apparatus can cause pain.

TOINETTE

Leave her alone.

SEAN

We're not here to leave each other alone.

TOINETTE

I want you to stop.

SEAN

A feeding apparatus can cause pain.

TOINETTE

That's enough.

SEAN

When does self-sacrifice become a fetish?

TOINETTE

That's enough.

SEAN

We're just talking. We're exploring the issues. There are issues here. When does a tender act become an obsession? Even abnormal in a way. Even morbid in a way.

TOINETTE

I told you. Stop.

SEAN

I don't have to listen to you. You're not my stepmother anymore. She's my stepmother now.

Scene 10

Toinette, Sean and Lia. Wine in small squat goblets, a bottle nearby. Lia, not drinking, sits slightly apart, nearer the sitting figure of Alex, who is upright in his chair, eyes open.

TOINETTE

First time I was here. By noon of the third day.

SEAN

You knew you were lost in space.

TOINETTE

I thought I was disappearing. Third day was the last day. I felt transparent. I think I actually panicked. I felt a kind of spiritual panic. I'm exaggerating.

SEAN

Just the two of you.

TOINETTE

He and I.

SEAN

What did you talk about?

TOINETTE

I don't know. Everything. Plants. Late the first night, he got going on the subject of plants. He loved the names of desert plants. He went into little whirling ecstasies. Reciting, you know, name, type, genus, species.

SEAN
Larkspur.

TOINETTE
Larkspur. Where did the names come from? Not the scientific names—the common names. He thought there was something inevitable in these names. They don't seem made up.

SEAN
Barrel cactus. Jumping cholla.

TOINETTE
He was almost ready to believe that the landscape and the names happened together.

SEAN
Fairy duster. Indian paintbrush.

TOINETTE
You know this. How do you know this?

SEAN
It's my job.

TOINETTE
What?

SEAN
To know everything he knew.

34

LIA
Navajo tea.

TOINETTE
Navajo tea. You too.

LIA
Paloverde. Apache plume.

TOINETTE
He went into little raptures, reciting the names. I can't remember a single one, not one, maybe one.

SEAN
Joshua tree. You remember Joshua tree.

TOINETTE
I remember larkspur.

LIA
Parish larkspur. Hides its nectar in the spur of the flower to protect it from insects that aren't honest-to-god pollinators. Bumblebees are okay. And they like the color blue. And larkspurs are blue. And bumblebees are strong enough to push apart the petals and get at the nectar. It all works.

SEAN
Night-blooming cereus.

LIA
Desert mariposa.

TOINETTE
And it's all one running creation. This is the thing he kept saying. The names as well. For those who know them.

SEAN

Brown-eyed evening primrose.

LIA

Sacred datura.

SEAN

Sounds awesome, doesn't it?

TOINETTE

Sacred datura.

SEAN

Insects get drunk on the nectar. People have visions. Fall down and weep.

LIA

Fall down and die. Can be fatal if you're not a hawkmoth.

TOINETTE

You both know this and I don't. We talked half the night. He belonged here. His mother was a westerner. Did you know that? He came out here when he was seventeen but had to go back east to live and work and study and paint and have wives. There was another one, you know.

LIA

Another one.

TOINETTE

Another wife.

LIA

Before you.

TOINETTE

And after me. Before you. You aren't number three. You're number four. Number three fled with her nightgown ablaze. He finally figured out that he couldn't escape himself with other people, another person. Another person made things worse. We made things worse, you and I. You didn't, I did. He thought he'd face the situation, head-on, alone, out here. Of course he didn't in the end. Because he couldn't.

LIA

Let's not analyze.

TOINETTE

I think we talked till dawn. I like these goblets. Five, six, seven years ago. Mountain standard time. Plants, trees, grasses, shrubs. Breathtaking genius in the names, he said.

SEAN

Sweetbush.

LIA

Brittlebush.

SEAN

Scarlet four o'clock.

LIA

Love-lies-bleeding. We went to India. He wanted to see the caves. It was the only trip we ever took together. The cave temples of Ajanta, unforgettable—sculptured, painted caves. And we were on a bus, and we were nearly there, and we saw a field of amaranthus, a type of amaranthus, and he told me the common name. Love-lies-bleeding. Slender red flowers. Spiky flowers.

SEAN

Who was the poet who thought of the name?

LIA

So beautiful. Cuts like a knife.

Toinette refills her glass again.

TOINETTE

Shoots like a gun. He shot himself, you know. We were living downtown, in a borrowed loft. Middle of the night, bang. I jump out of bed and he's sitting at the other end of the loft, half a block away, at the kitchen table, bleeding, and I was angry about this, and I stood by the bed, I didn't go to him, I stood where I was and I said, like, Shit what happened?

He said, I shot myself in the arm.

I said, How could you shoot yourself in the arm?

He said, How could I shoot myself in the leg?

I said, *Did* you shoot yourself in the leg?

He said, You miss the fucking point, Toinette.

He hated my name. He called me Toilette for a year and a half.

(To Alex.) Stupid shit.

(To Lia.) He had a gun. He owned a gun all the years I knew him.

SEAN

Shot himself accidentally.

TOINETTE

I don't know. I guess. I don't remember much else. I remember standing by the bed. I'm still standing by the bed. I'll always be standing there. Alex will always be bleeding at the other end of the loft. I was working for Time-Life then, fact-checking.

38

(Pause.) This is what he said. He said they didn't create the names of plants. They discovered them, like explorers, like Magellan discovering whatever he discovered. What was it Magellan discovered?

SEAN
The Strait of Magellan.

TOINETTE
What a lovely coincidence.

LIA
I need to get him to bed now.

TOINETTE
Let's get him to bed. I'll help you. Sean, get the wheelchair. I'll help you put him to bed if that's okay.

LIA
That's fine. Of course.

TOINETTE
Sean, get the wheelchair.

Sean does not move.

SEAN
I haven't looked at the stars yet. I need to go outside and do that.

Sean does not move.

Scene 11

The next day. Toinette, Sean and Lia. The sitting figure, head flung back and to one side, mouth wide open, eyes shut.

LIA

If he'd wanted to die, he would have done it himself. There was time for this. He was sick and weak but able to do things and able to understand what was ahead. This was ahead.

SEAN

He tore many connections. *(In Alex's voice.)* I tore many connections.

LIA

But not to life. Not everyone wants to choose the time. There's another level and that's what he chose. Die in nature's time. Yield to nature.

SEAN

Nature. Does anyone know what that is? I see polyethylene tubes that carry a chemical solution. You're protecting him from nature.

TOINETTE

He may be suffering.

LIA

Even if they said this. We can talk to a dozen doctors and lawyers. Discuss the physiology, the ethics, everything. The criminal statutes. Would they agree? And even if they did agree. All of them.

SEAN

He is suffering.

LIA

Even if they said this. All of them. He is suffering. Do you know what I would say? Let him suffer.

SEAN

Let him suffer.

LIA

He has the right to suffer. This is what being in the world means. At times we suffer.

TOINETTE

What do you know about being in the world?

LIA

I know it's the world you made. Tend to the body. Manage the body. Alter the body. I'm not some kind of primitive. I try to think about what I'm doing. Be sure the body dies without discomfort, whether it's ready or not. He's not ready. He didn't end his life and he didn't ask me to end it for him.

TOINETTE

If he'd asked.

LIA

He signed no document. He made no statement.

SEAN

But if he'd asked.

LIA
I don't know.

TOINETTE
Would you have done it?

LIA
I don't know.

Scene 12

Toinette and Sean. The sitting figure, as in previous scene.

SEAN

I have the means. I have what we need. I wouldn't have come empty-handed, would I?

TOINETTE

But I'm thinking the tube. Can't we just remove it?

SEAN

Might take him—I don't know. Ten days to die. Are you willing to wait?

TOINETTE

Ten days.

SEAN

I don't know—two weeks. He'd last a month without food. Take away his water, two weeks. And we'd have to deal with her. We remove the tube, she reinserts it.

TOINETTE

Even if we get her to agree, we can't sit here and wait.

SEAN

I did a great deal of waiting. I experienced waiting the way other people experience the thing they've waited for. It was the central fact.

TOINETTE

All right.

SEAN

Waiting to see him. Waiting for him to show up. Waiting for his mood to improve. Waiting for him to say something.

TOINETTE

All right.

SEAN

Other people wait, then do the thing they'll eventually remember. I remember the waiting.

TOINETTE

Look, fool. He wasn't going to stay with your mother. No matter what. I was the one, okay. But the marriage was dead. You know that.

SEAN

What did I know? I was unborn.

TOINETTE

But you've come to know that. I didn't force the breakup. We've said all this.

SEAN

I was curled up in my pouch. I was floating. I had gills and fins.

TOINETTE

We're joined, you and I, aren't we?

SEAN

Yes.

44

TOINETTE

It's important, this friendship.

SEAN

Yes, it is.

TOINETTE

We're also trapped in a way. Stuck with each other because of him, and stuck with him, and now with this, and it's the gravest sort of responsibility.

SEAN

Yes. One in which we have to bypass the feeding tube because it does us no good, in or out.

TOINETTE

You have the means.

SEAN

Of course.

TOINETTE

If he were conscious, if he could tell us what he wants. He wants the Nembutal, the Seconal, the applesauce. I know what I want. I want to go home.

SEAN

No, you don't. I need you here.

TOINETTE

The marriage was over. It was dead matter, with or without me.

SEAN

Then stop feeling guilty.

TOINETTE

What would you live on? Food and water? That's what he lives on. Look at him. I want to get out of here, now. But we can't leave him this way.

SEAN

He could be here for years.

TOINETTE

Years.

SEAN

Persistent vegetative state. Ten years, fifteen years. Longer. He could outlive you.

TOINETTE

Nice.

SEAN

I'll go to your funeral and then come here and tell him about it.

TOINETTE

Very nice. Funny.

SEAN

Because he can hear every word we say.

Scene 13

Sean and Lia. The sitting figure, head raised, eyes open. Lia moistens his lips with a soft cloth.

SEAN

Everything feels different. Even the room, the sort of room tone, the air in the room. You know this as well as I do. We know the same things now. Time, finally, to do something.

LIA

You can go home. That's what you can do.

SEAN

He's my father. This is his house. I know how hard it is for you. I know something else. Your resistance has worn away. It had to. Because you understand there's no true argument for keeping him here with you. You've always known this. The time had to come, that's all, when you stop resisting what you know. This is his death. Let him take it and leave.

LIA

You're well-prepared. But you haven't told me what a compassionate act we'd be performing. How we'd be partners in compassion. I've been waiting to hear that word so I can go and be sick somewhere.

SEAN

We need to be released, all of us. He's sitting here and he's holding us back. Our lives can't go forward. We love him. But it doesn't advance any cause, or deepen any loyalty, if he lives and breathes and goes on living and breathing. He may be sitting here ten years from now and we'll still love him, and we'll be the lesser for it. We'll be suffocated by his living. Not that he's alive. Not that he's dead. No longer and not yet. This is where he is. Try to understand. It's not only us. He needs to be released.

LIA

You're so well-prepared, so eager to do this thing.

SEAN

You want to believe he's there, somewhere, in that sitting figure. But he isn't. There's no one there. He can't recover the slightest shred of identity. His eyes are cold ash. No longer and not yet. It's wrong to keep him suspended. Do the hard thing, out of love, not despair. Let the man die.

ACT TWO

Alex and Toinette, six years before the main action of the play.

Alex in vigorous health, Toinette travel-weary. The room is open to late-afternoon light, a sense of blazing sky, revealing colors and objects not clearly visible in the dimmer setting of Act One. A Navajo saddle blanket, a couple of ceremonial jars. There is also a tray with water glasses, wine goblets, bottles.

He is studying her.

TOINETTE
Tell me what you're looking at.

ALEX
Another lifetime.

TOINETTE
Sounds like my day. Began so long ago I was wearing pigtails.

ALEX
I'm looking at eleven years. That's how long we lasted, isn't it?
Long time. Or not so long. Seemed long, didn't it?

TOINETTE
Two airports, two airplanes, one piteous little car. You didn't
tell me to get four-wheel drive. Half of me is still in the car. I
had no idea you were so far from anything.

51

ALEX

What's anything? I have friends who visit. Serious people. They think I'm here to find peace of mind. The age-old idiot whimsy.

TOINETTE

I know why you're here.

ALEX

I'm just here. In winter the sharp-shinned hawk comes down to the scrub. I can sit and watch a hawk in a tree for unnumbered hours. I'm on his time. He don't move, I don't move. I drive out to the site and stay four, five days at a time. Work and sweat. Talk Spanish to my crew.

TOINETTE

I want to see what you're doing.

ALEX

We're moving rock. I drink water all day. Sweat and piss. Nothing in my head but what's in plain view.

TOINETTE

You're making it sound simpler than it is.

ALEX

I make things sound simpler than they are. That's what I do. The hawk hits a cactus wren and the little bird explodes.

TOINETTE

I want to see the work.

ALEX

No, you don't.

TOINETTE
Then why did I come here?

ALEX
To see me. The way I wanted to see you. Isn't it the most natural thing, a man and woman getting back in touch? Don't you
feel the erotic rumblings?

TOINETTE
I wasn't surprised to hear from you. Which is odd, considering
how long it's been. But I didn't expect to hear that you're
alone.

ALEX
Being alone is my punishment.

TOINETTE
For what?

ALEX
For everything. For this. For wanting exactly this.

TOINETTE
And then failing at it. Because be assured. It's only a matter of
time.

ALEX
Before what.

TOINETTE
You get married again.

ALEX
Is that right?

TOINETTE
How long am I staying?

ALEX
I don't know. Not long.

TOINETTE
I think we have two days of mutually assured tolerance. Three at most.

ALEX
What's your money like?

TOINETTE
My money. How strange that sounds.

ALEX
What do you do?

TOINETTE
Edit children's books for a small shaky imprint. We share a secretary.

ALEX
But you do all right. You get around.

TOINETTE
She brings her baby to work.

ALEX
Theater, dinner parties. Date distinguished older men. What else?

TOINETTE
Younger men with problems.

ALEX

How many doctors do you go to? For how many parts of your body? I picture you.

TOINETTE

Go ahead.

ALEX

Walking up Park Avenue. Doctors to your left, doctors to your right. Then over to Fifth. The big new so-and-so show at the Met. Flags and banners. Maybe a private screening in the evening, downtown. Same seven people you saw the night before. Isn't this cancer-causing?

TOINETTE

A couple of years ago I had to sell one of your paintings.

ALEX

You didn't get rich doing that.

TOINETTE

I kept some of your paintings. I was desperate to have them. I needed them nearby. I wanted you breathing from the walls. You have foundation support, yes?

ALEX

Won't last nearly as long as I'll need it. I don't attract that kind of commitment. You never had much money, did you? And you could never figure out how that happened. Because you were supposed to have money, somehow, in your mind, from some-where. You looked like money.

TOINETTE

What do I look like now?

ALEX

Sex.

TOINETTE

That's not so bad.

ALEX

That's not so bad.

TOINETTE

I was twenty-two, you bastard.

ALEX

We were all twenty-two. We were all forty-two. What are you
talking about?

TOINETTE

I like these goblets.

ALEX

They're goblets.

TOINETTE

But why do they look familiar?

ALEX

I don't know. Why?

TOINETTE

They're mine. That's why.

ALEX

They're goblets.

TOINETTE

I was the second wife. This is supposed to be the beginning of the stunted male's maturity. But you weren't stunted exactly. You weren't unfinished or unshaped. I was the unfinished one.

ALEX

Do you know what I miss? I miss the subway.

TOINETTE

(Strong male voice.) Stand clear of the closing doors, please.

A pause indicating a passage of time. Light changes as sunset approaches. Alex sits close to her now.

TOINETTE

I was the one person you talked to, ever, about anything that mattered. Now I talk to Sean. He's living somewhere in Pennsylvania. You're not interested in this. Teaching at a private academy for rich kids who deal drugs. He calls me up, all hours. How angry does it make you, knowing that he and I talk? You're ready to rip me apart. I'll tell him that. There's no moment too fleeting for Sean. He wants to hear everything. The little cookbook of human motive. Your rages, my betrayals. Or lack of motive. Unknown motive. The near nightly drama of Alex murderously brooding. You brooded on things. You blamed me for things. You developed elaborate brooding theories. You blamed me for the art world, everything and everybody in it. Sean listens. I see him in a small tidy room, listening. I withhold things from him. I make him beg a little. The time you rode the Staten Island Ferry, back and forth, all day and into the night, for how many days straight, coming home to do some coke—ten days, maybe twelve. We don't talk often but we talk. Sean and I. It's talk on the level of heartbreak TV. We talk because you're rooted in our lives. We're too weak to let you go, or too hollow.

Let's face it, you wouldn't be worth the time otherwise. I'm not sure how it works but men who don't know themselves have a power over others, those who try miserably to understand. I owe him something, your son. I owe him roughly half a life.

ALEX

I always thought I'd kill someone. I don't know why it didn't happen. I think I wanted it to happen. No, not a woman. No matter what a woman did, you or anyone. Had to be a man. Had to be some dim rage, some dimwit fucking fury where you want to hammer somebody into the concrete. Being alone. It feels right to me, being here. But hard, but deadly at times. Women saved me from this. But look what happened. You saved me, you turned my life. But look what happened to us. We were hooked into each other. We had the same smell. We had the same bad breath. We said everything two people can say, day and night. The only escape was sex. For you, that meant other men. For me, that meant you. You were like smoke. I closed my eyes and walked on through, sweet and easy. Being alone. I see myself all the time. Something bears in on me. Who I am, that's what it is, and there's no end to it. *(Pause.)* Could be anybody. A guy you bump into turning a corner. You brush against. A guy you brush against and you don't like the look he gives you. You want to take his face and smash it. I ought to feel lucky it didn't happen. But here I am, paying for it anyway.

TOINETTE

Where is the site? Tell me.

ALEX

Mountains about thirty miles west of here. Gravel road, then a dirt track. I have three men working. Drilling and dynamiting. There were five but two pulled out.

58

TOINETTE

Blasting a space of some kind. Out of rock.

ALEX

A room, a cube. I don't have a name for it. First we cut a passage in. A rough narrow entranceway, cramped, with jutting rock.

TOINETTE

I make my way through a cold, dank, narrow space.

ALEX

Fifty meters. Natural light only. Bring a flashlight, I guess.

TOINETTE

I reach the end. What do I find?

ALEX

A chamber, a cubical room. Fashioned out of solid rock. Precise dimensions. A large empty room. Six congruent square surfaces. Painted. Ocher and amber. Old colors. Burnt brick. Lampblack. All six surfaces, every square inch.

TOINETTE

Painted.

ALEX

Painted.

TOINETTE

And the paintings. What do I see exactly?

ALEX

You understand this will never happen. It'll never get that far. I don't want to describe the paintings anyway. Wouldn't be able to.

TOINETTE

I think I know them.

ALEX

Is that right?

TOINETTE

Yes, I know the paintings.

ALEX

How is that possible?

TOINETTE

You talked about them. Once or twice only. Middle of the night, we're in bed, smoking, with the cat on the windowsill, watching.

ALEX

You remember this.

TOINETTE

Art that's hidden in a mountain. An incredible, you said, sort of stone enclosure that you would drench with paintings of your dreams.

ALEX

I said this. And the cat.

TOINETTE

You used to write down your dreams. Your analyst made you do this. You were crazy, I wasn't. But we both had analysts.

ALEX

Mine died on me.

TOINETTE

I laughed so hard.

ALEX

It'll never be finished. Years of work ahead. I don't have the resources. Site too remote. Access too difficult. That's one thing. There's another. Should the room be painted at all? I have my doubts. I always have my doubts. The paint's a mistake. The paint is excess. A bare room inside a mountain. I trust what's real. Rock. You can't socialize it. But why do I think there's something sad and frail in this work? You think I'm crazy but I'm not crazy enough. I want to throw off doubt, stop thinking, stop caring, just be, just work. Throw off who I am, goddamn it. A bare room without a signature. Just there. Except it won't be there.

A pause indicating a passage of time. The room is radiant in last light.

TOINETTE

There we were. We smoked, we talked.

ALEX

Remember what we used to say. I find myself thinking about this, out of nowhere. When we were in bed, at certain greedy moments. But other times, too. Sarcastically, in anger. Or just joking around.

TOINETTE
Make me come.

ALEX
A little smeary moan. Sometimes at dinner, with people.

TOINETTE
Big bright faces bobbing and weaving.

ALEX
I'd catch your eye and we'd whisper across the table.

TOINETTE
We'd mouth the words.

ALEX
Mouth the words. Curious words, when you think about it.

TOINETTE
Make me come.

ALEX
Like a child learning to speak.

TOINETTE
You fell in love with the word *gravlax*.

ALEX
That's very funny.

TOINETTE
You titled a painting.

ALEX

That's very funny. I don't remember that.

TOINETTE

Didn't you title a painting?

ALEX

Gravlax.

TOINETTE

It's only a matter of time. You won't be content to live with the woman you live with. You'll have to marry her. Because you need a structure. You want something organized and institutional. It's part of your confusion.

ALEX

You know this. You see into my mind and heart.

TOINETTE

I know why you're here. Risk everything. There's no safety here. It's all one thing. The art, the artist, the landscape, the sky.

ALEX

M'illumino d'immenso.

TOINETTE

I think we're ready to do some serious civilized drinking. Pour, please.

ALEX

M'illumino d'immenso.

TOINETTE

What's that?

ALEX

A line from a poem. Or the whole poem. I'm not sure.

TOINETTE

M'illumino.

ALEX

M'illumino d'immenso. I glow, I shine, I bathe myself in light. I turn luminous in this vast space. *D'immenso.* This vast space, this immensity. Fairly literal translation.

TOINETTE

Needs work.

ALEX

Okay, what?

TOINETTE

M'illumino d'immenso. I bathe myself. That's not bad. But vast space, vast space.

ALEX

D'immenso.

TOINETTE

Do we want space in the physical sense? Or spiritual immensity? Something unnameable.

ALEX

Let's not get too ambitious. We'll keep it local. This space and this light.

TOINETTE

So open it up a little.

ALEX
M'illumino d'immenso.

TOINETTE
I bathe myself in the light of this vast, this great, this what. We
need something to stretch the line.

ALEX
Some wine.

Alex pours.

TOINETTE
I got up at five a.m. No space, no light. *M'illumino.*

ALEX
M'illumino.

TOINETTE
I bathe myself in the light.

ALEX
D'immenso.

He is looking intently at Toinette.

TOINETTE
I bathe myself in the light of this epic desert space.

ALEX
Hey.

TOINETTE
M'illumino d'immenso.

ALEX

I bathe myself in the light of this epic desert space.

TOINETTE

I don't like it. Tell me what you're looking at.

ALEX

You know what I'm looking at.

TOINETTE

I was so damn young.

ALEX

Yes, you were.

TOINETTE

What happened?

ACT THREE

Scene 1

The dim interior of the room. Present time.

The sitting figure of Alex. The intravenous stand and feeding tubes are gone. He is wearing a different pair of shoes—plain brown oxfords. His eyes are closed, head slumped.

Lia sits next to him.

There is a bottle of dark liquid on a table nearby. It stands on a plain manila folder.

Sean is standing stage right. When Lia sees him, she gets to her feet.

SEAN

This is what will happen. I will apply the substance under the tongue. I will measure it out slowly and carefully. I will do it slowly so he doesn't choke. And I will do it in an even sequence of doses to avoid other side effects. I know it is stupid to speak of side effects under the circumstances. I will apply a few drops at a time. His system will absorb them and he will begin to fade.

LIA

I don't want to be here when this is happening. I'll go walking. I haven't done that in a while.

SEAN

I was out early. I walked all the way to that lonely fencepost on the old telephone trail. The heat's already brutal. Take a hat.

LIA

Do you know how long it will take?

SEAN

I will count the milligrams and listen to his breathing. His breath will go shallow. The idea is to maintain a certain pace. There has to be a balance. Do you need to be alone with him a while longer?

LIA

I was with him through the night. I think we're ready.

SEAN

Take some water with you.

They embrace.

Scene 2

Toinette and Sean. The sitting figure, as in previous scene. Sean holds the manila folder.

TOINETTE
I know what you're going to say. Don't say it.

SEAN
All right.

TOINETTE
It wasn't a dream. And I wasn't hearing things.

SEAN
You were hearing Lia. She was with him. She spoke to him.

TOINETTE
I can't identify the voice. But it wasn't hers. A voice speaking. Not a house sound, or wind, or mice in the walls. A voice speaking words.

SEAN
Don't do this to yourself.

TOINETTE
I think I heard him in the night.

SEAN

It was a matter of time. Someone had to hear him in the night.
It had to be in the night.

TOINETTE

I believe it happens. There are cases where people. After years
actually.

SEAN

Don't embarrass yourself.

TOINETTE

I wanted her so badly to be with us. Now that she is—I don't
know.

SEAN

You feel yourself maybe wavering a little.

TOINETTE

I'm still totally, emotionally bound.

SEAN

Do you want me to tell you I can do it alone?

TOINETTE

No. Just tell me what you want me to do.

SEAN

Be strong. And listen. (*He takes some papers from the folder and
reads.*) "Sublingual morphine is an effective route of adminis-
tration at end of life when patients can no longer swallow."

TOINETTE

All right.

SEAN

Listen. *(He reads.)* "If dosage is escalated substantially above recommended levels because of tolerance development, convulsions may occur in individuals even if they have no history of convulsive disorders."

TOINETTE

All right.

SEAN

A high dosage over a short period of time is risky for that reason. A seizure would be awful to witness and to deal with. A gradual dosage works better and it's also less clearly traceable.

TOINETTE

I was hoping we wouldn't have to approach that subject at all.

SEAN

The fact is this. Doctors do this all the time. They use a morphine drip. I don't know how to do this properly and I don't know how long it would take. But doctors everywhere do this. Trust me. They increase morphine dosage in the name of pain reduction. In fact they are hastening the moment of death. It's called terminal sedation and it's an act of mercy.

TOINETTE

How do you know what the dosage ought to be?

SEAN

(Waving a page.) "Dosage is a patient-dependable variable." But there are indications here about how to proceed.

TOINETTE

I know this is not interesting—but. Where did you get the morphine?

SEAN

This is not interesting.

TOINETTE

All right. But here's something interesting. Have you done this before?

SEAN

No.

TOINETTE

No.

SEAN

This is interesting. But no.

TOINETTE

Tell me what you want me to do.

SEAN

I want you to stand behind him. One hand to each side of his mouth. Use your fingers to sort of push the mouth open. I have a syringe. I think it's a child's syringe. I will wedge it under the tongue. And I will depress the plunger very gently so that the liquid does not splash out of the mouth.

Neither person moves toward the sitting figure.

TOINETTE

These pages you've been reading from.

SEAN

The Internet.

TOINETTE

You gathered this material on your computer.

SEAN

Before I came out here. I went online.

TOINETTE

But wouldn't it also help to talk to a doctor?

SEAN

Just us. This is what she wants. His family, such as it is.

TOINETTE

When do we start?

Sean takes a small syringe out of his pocket.

SEAN

I want you to stand behind him.

Toinette approaches the sitting figure.

One hand to each side of the mouth.

She stands behind the figure.

Sort of push in on the cheeks so the mouth opens.

She puts her hands to his face and carefully raises his head. Sean takes the bottle from the table and removes the lid. He inserts the small syringe into the liquid.

Five milligrams. A few drops at a time. Then five more. Slowly and gently. Then again and then again. An even sequence of doses. Then we have an interval, an extended waiting period.

He stands a few feet from the sitting figure.

Then we do it again. And then again.

Scene 3

Sean and the sitting figure of Alex, head raised, eyes open. Bottle of morphine one-quarter diminished.

SEAN

I know it isn't true, what Lia says. She says that you can hear us. You can feel and think. You react, you're aware. I don't believe it. But even if I thought you could hear me, what would I say to you? I don't think I know what to say. I never did. I know what you would say if you could speak, if you chose to speak freely, in the spirit of little miracles. You would say, Not everything we feel has to be expressed, or can be expressed. We withhold some things. Some things are too powerful, or too breakable. We withhold, we suppress, we whisper. We're free to do this, you would say. We whisper to our lovers. Why? Because some things are too precious to enter the world. Because too much can be said. Because love can't bear all this saying. But what about the son who sits in a room with his father? What happens then? I don't know. It was never clear to me who I was supposed to be in your presence. You were fixed forever within yourself. I was outside somewhere, watching us both. Not that I don't understand. I understand. Being a father had nothing to do with you. Having a child. It was an encroachment of the worst sort. It violated your seclusion, your private turmoil. I was proud of you. Did you know that? Proud to be the son of an artist. The cold-blooded bastard is a painter in a studio. That one day, I was twelve years old, standing in a corner to watch you work. Acrylic on masonite. Hearing those fantastic words.

Painting made sense to me, abstract painting made sense to me. It was acrylic on masonite. And cold black coffee in a paper cup. I drank some of your coffee and nearly fell down dead.

Sean takes a seat near his father.

All right, here's a joke. It's a philosophical joke. I told it to my seniors in geophysics. Goes like this. Two tiny young fish are swimming in the sea. They come upon an older fish. He says to them, Hey, fellas, how's the water? The two young fish swim on past. They swim for many miles. Finally one fish says to the other, What the fuck is water?

Sean studies his father.

It's a philosophical joke. What the fuck is water? *(Pause.)* In time I knew what I wanted. I wanted to look a certain way and sound a certain way. I worked at things. I trained myself to think a certain way. We were scared, weren't we, both of us.

77

Scene 4

Toinette and Sean. She stands behind the sitting figure, holding his head upright. His eyes are closed. Sean is seated, holding the computer pages.

SEAN

Listen to this. *(He reads.)* "Overdosage with morphine is characterised by respiratory depression, i.e., a decrease in respiratory rate and/or tidal volume, and also by Cheyne-Stokes respiration and cyanosis." They spell *characterised* with an *s*.

TOINETTE

It's been four hours and the breathing is the same.

SEAN

But cyanosis. Do you know what that is? Skin turns blue. This is something we can watch for. *(He reads.)* "Extreme somnolence, skeletal muscle flaccidity, cold and clammy skin, and sometimes bradycardia and hypotension."

TOINETTE

It's been four hours.

SEAN

I love the language of body failure.

TOINETTE

Are we sure four hours is the proper interval?

SEAN

If we want to avoid the grisly side effects.

Sean gets up, begins to fill the syringe.

TOINETTE

How many four-hour intervals before it's over?

SEAN

There's another matter. That's the morphine itself. This is not a recent prescription. The morphine is not recent. The bottle itself is not the original bottle. I think the expiration time for morphine is brief. Couple of years maybe.

He holds up the bottle.

Older the liquid, darker the color. The question is, Does morphine become more or less potent over an extended period of time? There may be some evaporation. This could increase potency. I've read a number of studies. There are no rules.

He places the syringe in the mouth of the sitting figure and depresses the plunger slowly.

I think this is a child's syringe.

A pause. He withdraws the syringe and looks at Toinette.

Where are you?

Momentary silence.

TOINETTE

Night-blooming cereus. That's one of them, isn't it?

SEAN
Yes, that's right.

TOINETTE
What else?

SEAN
Larkspur. You remember larkspur.

TOINETTE
My mind's so blank.

SEAN
Indian paintbrush.

TOINETTE
What else?

SEAN
Joshua tree.

TOINETTE
Do we know exactly what it is we're doing at this point?

SEAN
Joshua tree.

TOINETTE
Joshua tree.

SEAN
Scarlet four o'clock.

TOINETTE

Scarlet four o'clock. *(Pause.)* Navajo tea.

SEAN

Navajo tea. Yes, that's right, that's good. Desert mariposa. *(He looks at her and waits.)* Desert mariposa. *(He waits.)*

Scene 5

Room set is dark. Lights up on lectern, downstage, left, as in Act 1, Scene 7. Lia enters and takes up a position behind the lectern.

LIA

I don't know if it's customary for the wife to speak at a memorial service. The widow. But I came here to say that everything you may believe you know about Alex is only what you know, and it's not everything.

He was not the older man. I was not the younger woman. Can you understand that? The woman half his age, or whatever I was, or whatever he was. We never thought of each other as husband and wife. We were married but we never used those words or fit ourselves into them. I don't know what we were. We were one life, one pulse.

I understand now how two people can live together and when one of them dies, the other has to stop living. The other can't live a single day or a single week. A day may be passable, livable. A week, too long and dark. One dies, the other has to die.

I know people tell stories at these gatherings. I don't want to do that. People tell stories, exchange stories. I don't know any stories. You know things about him that I never knew. This means nothing to me. There are no stories. You're here for the wrong reason. If you're here to honor his memory, it's not his memory, it's your memory, and it's false. There are no stories. There are other things, hard to express, so deep and true that I can't share them, and don't want to. In the end it's not what kind of man he was but simply that he's gone. The stark fact. The thing that turns us into children, alone under the sky. When it stops being unbearable, it becomes something worse. It becomes the air we breathe.

My failure came at the end. He could have gone on, I could not. My weakness, my failure, this is what I carry. His life is what I carry, step by step.

He left in the arms of Morpheus, god of dreams.

I've come all this way to say these things. You'll leave and forget what I've said and so will I. I'll go back home and climb into the burning hills, where he worked, and scatter his ashes there. He goes nowhere now, into nothing. What powerful work he had it in mind to make. Untitled, unfinished. But not nothing.

Scene 6

Toinette and Sean. The sitting figure, head slumped. Toinette, exhausted, sits on the sofa amid the litter of computer pages, head also slumped. Sean stands stage right, holding a plastic bag and duct tape. The bottle of morphine is one-quarter full.

Toinette looks up.

TOINETTE
What are you doing?

SEAN
Nothing.

TOINETTE
We're not doing that.

SEAN
Every-four-hours was probably a mistake. Every-four-hours is pain relief, not end-of-life.

TOINETTE
We're not doing a plastic bag. She wouldn't agree to that, ever. And we're not going to do it without her knowledge. I'm not going to do it and neither are you.

SEAN
I brought it along as an extra measure, just in case. I went to the supermarket. I went down the aisle marked Foils and Wraps. I

84

bought turkey size. I did this with full understanding of the crushing absurdity of the moment.

TOINETTE
It wouldn't be you otherwise.

SEAN
Nineteen inches by twenty-three and a half inches. This is turkey size. I already had duct tape. Saved me a trip to the hardware store.

TOINETTE
We'll do what we've been doing, and we'll wait.

Sean approaches the sofa. He puts down the tape and plastic bag and sorts through the printouts, finding the one he wants.

SEAN
Listen to this. *(He reads.)* "Patients having chronic morphine therapy have been known—"

TOINETTE
Stop reading to me, please.

SEAN
Have been known. You won't believe this—"have been known to take in excess of three thousand milligrams a day with no apparent toxic effect being present."

TOINETTE
I can't listen to this.

SEAN
Intravenous is more effective. We're not interested in pain relief. We're interested in end-of-life.

TOINETTE

Can't listen, can't listen, can't listen.

SEAN

His skin should be showing some blue by now. The slightest little discoloration.

Sean takes the bottle and syringe. He fills the syringe and waits as Toinette gets up from the sofa and approaches the sitting figure. She stands behind the figure and raises his head, a hand to each side of his face.

TOINETTE

You've willed all this, haven't you? These few days—how many days has it been? Only two, I think, shaped and managed by force of will. You sort of maneuvered everything into this moment. Even, somehow, the things I've said.

SEAN

Even, somehow.

TOINETTE

All the conversations between the two of us and among the three of us. It's as though you've been leading up to this for years.

SEAN

It's as though.

TOINETTE

To punish us. Punish him and punish me.

SEAN

What language are you speaking? I want you to listen to yourself.

TOINETTE

This whole sequence of events. It's retaliation, isn't it? Not just him but me as well.

SEAN

It's all right. You're tired and a little crazy. I understand. And I'm going to think of something wise and loving to say. Give me a moment.

TOINETTE

I've lost count of the number of times we've done this procedure. I'm feeling not quite sure I'm completely here. I'm feeling vague. I have no sense of time. I don't think I slept last night. There were mice in the walls.

Scene 7

Lia sits next to the figure of Alex. She holds a soft cloth in her lap. The figure's head is raised, eyes closed.

The bottle of morphine is nearly empty.

A silence.

Toinette stands in a corner of the room.

TOINETTE
Has his breathing changed?

LIA
No.

TOINETTE
We'll be patient.

LIA
We'll hold his hand. Moisten his lips.

Toinette stands behind the sitting figure, a hand to each side of his face.

TOINETTE
His breathing will change. This is something we can listen for.

LIA
Where will you go when you leave?

TOINETTE

San Francisco. To stay with friends. Four or five days. Then back to New York.

LIA

I've never been to New York. So many places.

TOINETTE

They're not really friends. They're people I met somewhere, married forever. We keep in touch. I don't know why I'm going really.

LIA

Moisten his lips. Wipe his brow.

TOINETTE

We counted the milligrams. Drop by drop, under the tongue. There are no rules. When his breathing changes, we'll know it's nearly time. This is the sign we have to wait for.

LIA

Be patient.

TOINETTE

Be there with him.

LIA

Wait for him to fade.

TOINETTE

I wish I'd told them no. I'd like to go straight home. They're serious about tap dancing. They take tap-dancing lessons.

LIA

I walked for so long.

TOINETTE

I need to walk more. A thing I know I'll never do. One of the ten thousand things.

LIA

Sometimes I think there's no end to it. I walk and walk and it may look the same but it's not and it may look empty but it's not and there's nothing moving. I'm the only thing in motion, although there are countless other things, everywhere. It goes on and on. But now I sit here. I think, We're in a room, hidden away from all that sky and light, and this is where everything is.

TOINETTE

I trust you. I want you to tell me we're not fools.

LIA

Everything that matters is pressed between these walls. In this sickroom. And I don't know if I can bear it anymore.

Scene 8

Toinette and Sean. The sitting figure, as in previous scene, head raised, eyes shut. Toinette stands behind him, a hand to each side of his face. Sean is asleep on the sofa. The bottle of morphine is empty.

A silence.

TOINETTE
He stopped breathing.

Sean begins to stir.

I've been listening so hard. Concentrating. Waiting for his breathing to change. I thought it would go shallow. But this didn't happen. Or I just didn't hear it.

Sean sits up.

He stopped breathing. I don't know when it happened. I've been waiting and listening. I don't know how long I've been standing here. And I just this moment realized. He isn't breathing. He stopped. There's nothing.

Sean sits there, looking straight ahead.

Be patient, I thought. I thought, As long as someone's here. Someone has to be here when it happens. I tried so hard to listen. He isn't breathing, Sean. I don't know when it happened. *(Pause.)* Look at him. *(Pause.)* Look at your father.

Sean does not look.

Scene 9

*Alex and Lia, one year before the main action of the play, as in
Act 1, Scene 1. They are isolated from the room set, which is dark
except for a sliver of light on the sitting figure, feeding tubes not
visible. There is a bowl with food.*

LIA

But your memory of the man himself. Intact. The dead man.

ALEX

Nobody paid him the slightest mind. That's how my father
would say it. The slightest mind. He went to the track once or
twice a year. Most years maybe not at all. He followed the horses
in the newspaper. The Daily Mirror. He read the race results like
they were holy scripture.

LIA

And the man across the aisle. Intact. You can see him.

ALEX

I can nearly touch him.

LIA

You can see him so clearly, you said, that you feel you know
him.

ALEX

Sixty years ago.

LIA

Because I say to myself, What good is a life that doesn't experience some trace of all possible lives? What's the point of being only who we are? Isn't this the sort of unspoken limitation we live with, most of us, all the time? I mean shouldn't the man on the subway train, the man on a park bench who has no shoes, who's too beaten down even to beg, sitting there, so frail and soiled—shouldn't I be able to be in his life, be who he is, even for half a minute?

ALEX

Way too long.

LIA

It's not nearly enough.

ALEX

Half a second's all you need. Because all you have to do is walk past the bench.

LIA

Not nearly enough.

ALEX

Smell him.

LIA

Not enough.

ALEX

Human feces is so much more personal than dog shit. It tells you everything you need to know. It puts you in his life, shows you where the boundaries meet—his life and yours. That's why it's so hard to bear.

LIA

I can bear it.

ALEX

I know you can. I'm carrying around a corpse and we both smell him.

LIA

You can think and speak.

ALEX

Days go so quick. Days last ten minutes. It's always time to go to bed. It's always last night. I keep wondering how last night became tonight.

LIA

Your mind is strong.

ALEX

You want to experience a life remote from your own. Even for a moment. Some stray soul on a wet bench. I want to experience my own life. Everything's collapsing backwards. I can't feel what's here.

LIA

You can feel my hand on your body. That's what's here.

ALEX

You're the one blessing I know. All I can see and hear. The last of the body. There's more of you than there ever was of me. Everything's running backwards now. This is what consciousness is beginning to mean. Objects in rooms in dying light. I live in old objects, things turned gray. The photographs were always gray, along the narrow hall. The suits and dresses in the closet at the back of the house. My father wore a double-breasted suit with one lapel curled over. One floppy lapel. This is human consciousness. I live in the shoes braced by the shoe trees. In the hatboxes and the hanging belts.

LIA
You need to hold hard to life.

ALEX
If I take another blow. I know it's coming.

LIA
Your mind is alive.

ALEX
The most mysterious place in the world. My father and mother's closet. Mothballs and dusty secrets. Like church. This is what's left of me now. The lapel on my father's Sunday suit.

LIA
My hand on your body. This is what's left.

ALEX
My father was always scratching his back, or telling me to do it for him. People don't scratch their backs anymore. Itchy backs and forearms. Scratch my back, buster. He'd go into a semi-squat and I would scratch his back.

LIA
My breath on your face. That's what you feel and who you are, now, this instant. You need to hold hard.

A silence.

ALEX

Dan Parker. That was his name.

LIA

Whose name?

ALEX

The sportswriter. The columnist who wrote about the horses. Dan Parker. That was his name. They ran his picture in every column. This is the subway. I see the man's face in the little photograph. Dark hair. I see it very clearly. Dark shiny hair, slick mustache. It's burning a hole in my brain. *(Pause.)* Or is that my father? Is that my father who had the mustache?

LIA

You need to eat something now. Stay strong. This is what you need to do. First, eat something. Then we'll talk.

Scene 10

The sitting figure in isolation.
Black.